C000183474

RAILWAY MOODS

# THE WELSHPOOL & LLANFAIR RAILWAY

## MIKE HEATH

HALSGROVE

First published in Great Britain in 2006

Copyright: text and photographs © 2006 Mike Heath

*All rights reserved. No part of this publication may be reproduced, stored in a retrieval system, or transmitted in any form or by any means without the prior permission of the copyright holder.*

**British Library Cataloguing-in-Publication Data**
A CIP record for this title is available from the British Library

ISBN 1 84114 532 7
ISBN 978 1 84114 532 7

**HALSGROVE**
Halsgrove House
Lower Moor Way
Tiverton, Devon EX16 6SS
Tel: 01884 243242
Fax: 01884 243325
email: sales@halsgrove.com
website: www.halsgrove.com

Printed and bound by D'Auria Industrie Grafiche Spa, Italy

# INTRODUCTION

In the late nineteenth century the Banwy Valley farming communities' only link to the outside world was via the Cambrian Railway's station at Welshpool. Their businesses had been suffering because of the costly horse drawn transport carrying goods to, and supplies from, the station. The passing of the Light Railways Act in 1896 created circumstances whereby rural railways could be constructed more cheaply than before, resulting in a plethora of schemes being promoted all across the country. An Order authorising the Welshpool & Llanfair Railway was made on 8 September 1899. Construction of a 2ft 6ins narrow gauge railway between Welshpool Station and Llanfair Caereinion commenced in 1901, opening for freight traffic in March 1903, with the first passengers carried the following month. The line struggled to operate profitably and passenger services were withdrawn in 1931. Freight traffic continued beyond nationalisation in 1948 but the railway was destined for closure and the last train ran on 2 November 1956.

By this time the preservation movement which had started at the Talyllyn Railway in 1950, no doubt gave encouragement to the group of enthusiasts that set about saving this line. In 1962 following lengthy negotiations the Welshpool & Llanfair Railway Preservation Company Limited, which had been formed in 1960, was able to lease the line from British Rail.

An interesting and unusual feature of the original route was the section in Welshpool which actually ran through the town's streets. Unfortunately, this was excluded from the sale agreement and thus deprived the Company of the railway's original headquarters and operating centre. Another problem was that the original passenger stock had been systematically scrapped during the long freight-only operating period. But, as has been seen at centres all over the country, preservationists with limited funds were able to create opportunity from adversity. The operating centre and salvaged rolling stock, including the railway's two original locomotives, were relocated to Llanfair and over the years an extremely interesting collection of both locomotives and passenger coaches acquired from all over the world has been brought in to operate on the line. This has imparted a distinctly foreign atmosphere which complements this otherwise traditional Welsh rural railway recreation.

The line was reopened to Castle Caereinion in 1963 and to Sylfaen in 1972. Operations on the full 8 mile line to Welshpool recommenced on 18 July 1981 following completion of the new terminus at Raven Square.

Today visitors are taken on a journey that follows a steeply graded route through the rolling Welsh hills, follows a river valley, passing through farms and across farmland, traverses a viaduct and winds its way round a mill. At each road crossing the fireman disembarks to guard the way as the train passes over. It is a wonderfully serene and leisurely trip.

The line has been described as a gem in an area too often missed by the traveller passing through for further shores. Next time you are passing don't just call in, take a ride. I guarantee that you will not be disappointed.

# THE WELSHPOOL AND LLANFAIR RAILWAY

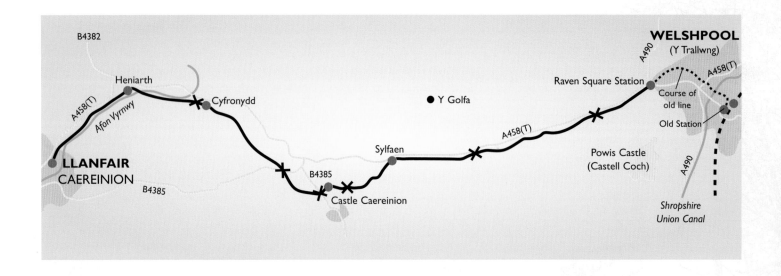

Our journey starts at Raven Square Station, Welshpool. In 1977, it having proved impossible to acquire the town section of the original line, an appeal was launched to rebuild the line from the then terminus at Sylfaen. Success came four years later with the first passenger train departing on 18 July 1981. The volunteers can take pride in the work that they did as they have created a very attractive station with excellent facilities providing a warm welcome for passengers.

Fortunately the railway has managed to preserve and operate the two original locomotives built for the line by Beyer Peacock & Co. at their foundry in Gorton, Manchester. Named in honour of the Earl and Countess of Powys in recognition of the support given by the Earl to the construction of the railway, both locomotives took charge of all traffic on the line from its opening in 1903 to closure in 1956. Here the first locomotive to arrive on the line in 1902, No. 822 *The Earl,* takes water ninety-eight years later!

*Opposite:* The second locomotive, No. 823 *The Countess* is seen taking water in its centenary year. Note the 'new' water tower which originates from the Pwllheli station of the Cambrian Railways, and was erected in 2001 to replace the original preservation era tank seen in the last photograph.

In order to cope with the passenger traffic of today additional locomotives are brought in from all over the world to assist *The Earl* and *The Countess*. The latest, and largest, of these is *Orion*. Built by Tubsize in Belgium it was delivered to the Jokioisten Railway, situated about 100 miles north-west of Helsinki, in Finland where it carried the number 5 and worked from 1948 until 1963. It arrived on the Welsh line in 1983, underwent an extensive overhaul and entered revenue-earning service in June 2000.

Locomotive No.14 was built for the Sierra Leone Railway in West Africa by the Hunslet Engine Company, Leeds in 1954. It worked in and around Freetown until 1975 and was destined for the scrap yard. Fortunately, at the eleventh hour, repatriation to the W. & L. rescued it and in 1979 it entered regular traffic on the Welsh line.

The station approach is often used by enthusiasts engaged in other areas of transport preservation to showcase their own superb exhibits.

It also provides an opportunity to capture interesting scenes such as this.

Photo: Karl Heath

Earlier in the day, with the watering complete, *The Countess* eases forward to run round the train as passengers start to board.

*Opposite:* Dusk on a Gala Saturday evening and the water tanks are replenished in readiness for the last trip back to Llanfair.

On Gala days locomotives exchange trains at Raven Square and here *Orion* has backed off the train that has just arrived from Llanfair whilst No.14 has coupled up to haul the return journey. Compare this photograph with that on page 9 and you will note a different livery. The crimson livery viewed here was carried from the early 1990s until 2003 when it emerged from the workshops in the blue livery seen previously.

An imminent departure set against an autumnal background.

The original three coaches which were built by R. J. Pickering of Wishaw were the only passenger stock that operated on the W. & L. between 1903 and 1931. This particular replica is modelled on the original No.2 coach which provided a small first class compartment for 10 persons, a guard's compartment near the middle and a third class section with seating for 26 people. At either end is a covered balcony. This superb replica was constructed by the Ffestiniog Railway Company at Boston Lodge and entered service in 2004.

*Opposite:* September 2004 and that year's Gala was blessed with superb sunny weather rendering the celebratory bunting particularly colourful. The coach immediately behind the locomotive is a replica of those built for the opening of the original line.

The journey begins as *The Earl* draws past the signal box which was constructed in 1982.

*Opposite:* All intended passengers are aboard the last Gala day departure from Welshpool. The light from the station platform lamps contrasts sharply with the dusk–darkening exhaust from the locomotive.

On leaving Welshpool the trains immediately face a stiff climb, at 1 in 35, the start of which can be seen to the middle right-hand side of this photograph.

A departure viewed from the hedgerow alongside the main A458 road which will follow the railway all the way to Llanfair, and which was of course the competition that eventually brought about the closure of the line.

Photo: Karl Heath

21

*Orion* continues to climb as the first open level crossing, at New Drive, is approached.

This location is clearly determined by the striking black and white lodge located on the Drive alongside the railway.

The next section sees the line winding its way through the trees as it temporarily veers away from the road and climbs steeply up Golfa Bank which includes a mile long section at a gradient of 1 in 29. The woods in the background are just a part of the Powys Estate and extend over the hillside as far as Powys Castle itself.

*Opposite:* As shadows lengthen, including those of myself and younger son Karl with cameras capturing the scene, *The Countess* powers over the crossing.

The train has now neared the top of the incline and is about to pause at Golfa Halt. Originally a loop had been provided here for goods traffic.

Cwm Lane, a very narrow minor route, used mainly by farm traffic, and the occasional photographer, runs across the line immediately alongside the halt. Here the fireman will leave the engine to guard the train across the lane.

Once safely across, the fireman will climb back aboard and the regulator will be opened as the journey continues the climb to the bank's summit. The first coach behind the locomotive is one of a number donated to the railway by the Zillertalbahn in the Austrian Tyrol. They are wooden bodied on steel underframes. The open balconies at each end and large opening windows have proved extremely popular with travellers. A trip on one of these is highly recommended.

*Opposite:* By coincidence, in 2005 my wife and I holidayed in the Austrian Tyrol at Jenbach, home of the Zillertalbahn and the opportunity was taken to ride on one of these coaches on the railway for which they were constructed. This photograph shows the Austrian locomotive coupling up to that day's 'Nostalgia Train' at Jenbach.

The Zillertalbahn runs south from Jenbach towards the Zillertal Alps and the ski resort of Mayrhofen. The pristine Tyrolean scenery through which the railway passes is clearly evident as the 'Nostalgia Train' heads back to Jenbach.

*Opposite:* Meanwhile back in the more rolling landscape of mid-Wales a former Zillertalbahn coach is tucked in behind *The Earl* as the journey up Golfa bank continues.

Photo: Karl Heath

You will no doubt have noted that the last photograph was taken by my son, Karl, one of a number taken by him and included in this album. One benefit of us sharing this hobby is that totally different views of the same train in the same location can be taken, as is the case here.

A little nearer the summit and the almost totally camouflaged train eases across the scene. I well remember that split-second timing was required for this shot as a car had just passed by and a second was about to enter stage right!

*Orion* approaches the summit. The train formation is of great interest as whilst the lead, Pickering replica, coach was in its first year of operation, the rear, former Zillertalbahn, coach had been carrying passengers for over a century.

*Opposite:* 2¾ miles into the journey is the first halt at Sylfaen. This was originally intended to just serve the nearby farms and a small siding was constructed for that purpose.

The Welshpool & Llanfair Light Railway 'Travellers Guide' tells that throughout its former life a box had been provided at the halt in which small parcels were left and a special blast on the locomotive whistle would alert the locals that they were available for collection. Oh how times have changed!

*Opposite:* The middle coach seen here is one of four on the railway which, although relatively young in comparison to the Austrian coaches, have an interesting international history of their own. They were built in Gloucester in 1961 and presented to Sierra Leone by the British Government to mark the former colony's independence. Only thirteen years later they formed the last train that ran marking the closure of the Sierra Leone Railway. They arrived on this line in 1975 along with locomotive No. 14 which by coincidence is hauling this train away from the halt.

Sylfaen is now only a halt except for times of intensive services such as Gala days when the loop, seen here on the left, is used for crossing trains.

Opposite: The late afternoon sun provides perfect lighting to capture a 'mixed train' comprising both passenger and freight stock as it continues west at the end of a Gala day afternoon in 1999.

With the Welshpool-bound train about to depart Sylfaen in the background, *The Earl* has passed through the loop and is hauling its mixed train towards the next station at Castle Caereinion

Same locomotive, same location, different train, cooler weather conditions. The first coach in this multi-national rake is one of two on the line that were built, in 1958, for one of the Hungarian State Railway's narrow gauge systems. They subsequently moved to the Ciernohronska Forest Railway in Slovakia where they remained until transferred to Wales in 1999.

The local farmer had recently harvested this field to ensure photographers a clear view of the passing Llanfair-bound train.

The line now climbs sharply to a second summit at 578 feet above sea level on the approach to Coppice Lane crossing which is a popular location for photographers. On 31 August 2002 a group of us were to be seen nervously waiting in the hope that the evening double-headed train would arrive before the rapidly-descending sun disappeared altogether.

It was touch and go!

No such problem on this occasion as *Orion* makes light work of a heavily-laden passenger service in May 2002.

*The Countess* will soon be slowing to around 5 miles an hour and whistling its arrival at the open level crossing.

*Opposite:* Once Coppice Lane has been crossed the line starts a winding descent before entering a deep cutting. This is the going-away shot of the double-headed train so anxiously awaited on the 31 August 2002.

After 3¾ miles the train emerges at Castle Caereinion Station. The village itself is located a quarter of a mile away up the hill behind the station.

The station boasts a loop, signal box and waiting room.  The signal box is a preserved survivor from the Cambrian era.

The signal box originally entered service in 1907 but was little used and in the 1930s ground frames (bottom right) were installed to operate the loop points reducing the box's duties to storage of permanent way tools. The use of ground frames has continued into the preservation era. A mixed train stands at the platform on a pleasant September evening.

*Opposite:* An authentic Welshpool & Llanfair goods train with suitably attired crew completing a timeless scene.

On leaving Castle Caereinion the line descends Dolarddyn Bank and another ungated level crossing is encountered as the line traverses the B4385, a secondary road to Llanfair. In this mid-winter view the train is accelerating away from the crossing.

*Opposite:* With the landscape in full bloom and the Welsh hedgerow-builder's 'Mark of Zorro' dominating the hillside *The Earl* drifts past the same location.

The journey continues towards Cyfronydd through sheep and cattle pastures with the hills and vales of mid-Wales providing a magnificent backdrop.

*Opposite:* Originally the station at Cyfronydd had a loop, gravel platform and simple waiting shelter with which it served Cyfronydd Hall on the hillside opposite and the village itself on the nearby main road.

Photo: Karl Heath

The little engine framed by the station signboard is *Dougal*. Built in 1946 by Andrew Barclay & Sons Co. Ltd in Kilmarnock it operated on the narrow gauge system around the Provan Gasworks of Glasgow Corporation until closure in 1958.

For many years the station was used by a local timber merchant and on Gala weekends the memories are rekindled as the siding again plays host to timber laden freight trains.

*Dougal* was saved from the cutters torch in 1961, arrived on the railway in 1969 and six years later was steamed for the first time in preservation. Its diminutive size prevents it from working the main trains, but on Gala weekends can be seen at the head of shuttle freight trains between Llanfair and Cyfronydd.

No. 10 *Sir Drefaldwyn* (which is Welsh for the County of Montgomery) started life as a tender engine in 1944 on the German Military Railways. It later worked on the Salzburg-Bad Ischl line and was rebuilt as tank engine by the Styrian Government Railway in 1957 for use on the Weiz to Ratten line. Little used there, it found its way to Wales in 1969. Here in 1999 it is seen heading away towards Llanfair. On the right is the renovated body of a former London & North Western brake-van, the veranda of which is used as a waiting shelter.

Photo: Karl Heath

The railway continues its descent and at this point runs parallel to the south bank of the River Banwy.

*Opposite:* Just before Heniarth the line turns and crosses over the river by means of a steel girder bridge 114 feet long made up of three spans. Like most water courses in the height of summer during long spells of dry weather the Banwy appears to be nothing more than a gentle stream, but periodically, over the years, the river has become a raging torrent and caused severe damage to the supporting stone piers. One such occasion in 1964 saw the destruction of the western side pier (left) which was replaced by a steel pier courtesy of the 16th Railway Regiment, Royal Engineers. More recently the whole structure has been re-decked and the Royal Engineers' pier has been encased in concrete and received a stonework facing as further protection.

Once across the river the line again comes into view from the main road high up on the right, from where this photograph was taken.

*Opposite:* For many years my interest in railway photography was shared by both my sons, although now the elder, Darren, no longer joins us on our trips. However, as mentioned earlier, Karl's enthusiasm for the subject remains strong and more often than not he disappears to find alternative locations to those chosen by myself.

Photo: Karl Heath

While Karl was taking this atmospheric picture of a Santa Special train rounding the curve at Heniarth, I was positioned trackside, on the opposite side of the railway capturing the previous shot.

*Opposite:* With a late summer mixed train service *The Countess* approaches the site of the former Heniarth Halt.

Bare trees and the seasonal headboard confirm that winter has arrived as excited children are returned to Llanfair after visiting Santa at Cyfronydd.

Originally known as Heniarth Gate, the halt originally had a loop line, waiting shelter, and crane for the loading of timber, serving the local farming community and the former water mill nearby. Nowadays there are no facilities at all and trains pass without stopping.

The train is now on the last leg of the journey to Llanfair as the line continues its riverside route towards Dolrhyd Mill, which is now used as a holiday cottage.

Photo: Karl Heath

*Dougal* scurries along with its timber cargo on a sunny Gala day.

This photograph dates from the 1999 Gala and shows No. 14 arriving at Llanfair as in the siding the newly restored *The Earl*, which had run under its own steam for the first time in twenty-one years just a couple of days earlier, idles the afternoon away.

The signal man prepares to receive the token from the crew of *Orion* as the train enters the Llanfair terminus. Taken in September 2000 when construction of the railway's new engine shed was underway and the original signal box was still in use.

Four years later and a new signal box has been constructed in the style of those seen at many places on the old Cambrian lines. With the replica Pickering coach in the formation *The Countess* arrives at the head of a mixed train recreating rural light railway travel of the 1920s.

A raised platform, over 100 yards long, was also constructed faced in blue bricks, the edgings surfaced with a diamond pattern, all of which were painstakingly reclaimed from several disused Cambrian stations including that at Welshpool.

All available locomotives operated that weekend including *Orion* which is seen here arriving under the watchful eye of the 'top hat and tailed' station master.

*Opposite:* In June 2003, as part of the railway's centenary celebrations, an Edwardian Weekend was held for which many working members turned out in superb period costumes. For a short time in the afternoon the platform was taken over by the volunteers dressed in the elegant fashions of a century ago. A very sharp contrast with the less tastefully clad photographers on the opposite side of the track!

The railway's two original locomotives stand side by side on the line for which they were constructed over 100 years before.

*Opposite:* The crew of *The Countess* release the locomotive from the coaches and prepare to run into the head shunt where they will no doubt take on water before running round the train for the return journey.

The Company took over very basic facilities at Llanfair and in 1993 set about rebuilding the various sheds that existed to provide a new booking office, shop and station buffet which, by the way, is well worth a visit.

Alongside the entrance to the station, the awning is a replica of those under which farm supplies would have been unloaded.

*The Countess* and *The Earl* in the head shunt at dusk.

Gala weekend photography evenings are what first attracted me to the railway and have never been a disappointment. Early evening images benefit from the last remnants of colour in the night sky…

…which when combined with a little floodlighting can produce splendid results.

*Opposite:* Not all the exhibits on show are rail mounted. A regular visitor is this steam road roller built in 1922 by Aveling & Porter and named *Lady Hesketh*

*Lady Hesketh* simmers alongside a Sentinel Steam Wagon that dates from 1931. Do not be misled by the sign over the bar, those are not beer barrels on the back of the wagon. The vehicle has been restored in the livery of Morris's of Shrewsbury a company that collaborated with the Sentinel Wagon Company to produce steam oils.

*Opposite:* Showman's Engine *The Leader* lights up the yard as revellers sample the draught ales available from the licensed bar behind.

No. 10 *Sir Drefaldwyn* completes the trio of steam powered transport types.

*Opposite:* An interesting comparison between rail and road steam traction.

*Opposite:* These Gala nights give the opportunity to experiment with photography. With the lights set up to illuminate the locomotives for the traditional front three-quarter portraits, a walk down the line has revealed the backs of the engines silhouetted against the floodlit steam-filled background. Care has been taken to position the camera to ensure that none of the lights are directly visible in the frame as this would result in flare and fogging of the transparency.

A busy yard scene as *Dougal* warms down after working the day's shuttle freight trains whilst the locomotive that has recently arrived, at the head of an evening mixed train, rests in the run round loop.

Gala night on 1 September 2001 saw *Orion* at rest in the yard. The blue tubs between the tracks are usually filled with coal to be lifted manually onto the footplate and emptied in the locomotive's bunker.

Another photograph taken from down the line, this time with the camera in the shadow of the water tower to exclude the glare of the floodlights.

Photo: Karl Heath

Each year the railway tries to provide a different scene for the assembled photographers to capture. On this occasion *Sir Drefaldwyn, No. 14* and *The Countess* have been lined up across the yard.

*Opposite:* For this rear three-quarter shot, of No. 14 and *Sir Drefaldwyn,* the camera has been positioned just above track level and in the shadow of the coal dock to obliterate all direct light sources. With steam bursting through the safety valves of both locomotives the result is particularly atmospheric.

Photo: Karl Heath

In 2002 the two original Beyer Peacock locomotives were similarly positioned.

*Opposite:* Little in the form of *Dougal,* and large in the form of *The Countess,* rest side by side outside the railway's workshop.

On a lovely September evening *The Earl* makes the acquaintance of *Lady Hesketh*. (I feel a novel coming on!)

*Opposite:* Meanwhile *The Countess* stands patiently by the signal box awaiting permission to enter the station yard with a night freight.

At the first Gala of the new millennium the line up comprised *No. 14*, *Orion* and *The Earl*.

*The Earl* takes water in the head shunt as *Orion* stands alongside the coal dock in the yard.

This photograph of *No. 10* in the head shunt is taken from under the canopy of the original corrugated iron booking office and waiting room which, now restored, is used as the Company's registered office.

Photo: Karl Heath

The Llanfair train at night.

At Llanfair Caereinion the creation of the new passenger facilities was carried out with great care to maintain the railway's heritage and, but for the double yellow lines and modern coffee advertisement, the visit of a 1928 Ford Model AA van, also in Morris's Lubricants livery, would have completed a timeless scene.

Scenes from the past are also recreated in the railway yard including the tradition of having a brew and a butty before tackling the unenviable, and seemingly single-handed, task of unloading the recently arrived freight train. To make matters worse it looks like the boss has just driven in as well!

The Edwardian Weekend in June 2003 saw the railway inspire memories of its *raison d'etre* with a demonstration of the transfer of goods from road to rail.

Dougal shunted an open wagon alongside a suitably laden vintage truck in the transfer siding and the goods depot porters set to work.

Photo: Karl Heath

There is a certain irony in this picture which pairs a humble horse and cart, the form of haulage replaced by the railway, with a representative of the road transport that ultimately brought about the railway's demise.

*Opposite:* Over the years the railway has played host to many other forms of steam transport and in 2004 a 1929 Sentinel DG4 tar-spraying wagon stopped by to join the party.

On this occasion, even though the weather was not at its best, I could not miss this opportunity. Where else could you capture working steam cars, wagons, tractors and locomotives all within the same photo frame?

In the railway's heyday wagons were loaded with timber from a sawyer's yard located beside the main road at Llanfair. So it is appropriate that a demonstration of a steam-driven saw bench was included as part of the centenary celebrations.

On the return journey *Dougal* squeezes past the former Dolrhyd Corn Mill. At this point the original plans for the railway indicated a route between the mill and the main road from where this photograph was taken. A last minute change, no doubt a cost cutting exercise, saw the line diverted along the narrow stretch of bank between the mill and the river.

*Opposite:* Man and machine in perfect harmony.

With the tightly curved section of track around the mill successfully negotiated, the little freight train scampers towards Cyfronydd.

Photo: Karl Heath

Even on a cool damp day the covered balconies of the passenger coaches are still the best way to sample the character and charm of this rural light railway and that unmistakable steam vapour.

The train has just passed the site of Heniarth Halt arousing the interest of the local livestock. In the background are the buildings of a former water mill which now serves as a private residence.

The low winter sun provides superb backlighting to a Santa Special train rounding the curve on the approach to the Banwy bridge.

Under a warm September sky *The Earl* passes the same point with a vintage mixed train.

The large windows of the ex-Zillertalbahn coach coupled to *The Countess* affords the passengers a clear view of a photographer up to his knees in water!

Photo: Karl Heath

Another Santa Special skirts the river across a landscape dappled in light and shadow.

It may be smokey, it may be noisy, but many passengers are keen to 'bag' the balcony next to the locomotive. Here the train is pulling in to the station at Cyfronydd which on December weekends prior to Christmas brings an increased level of excitement to the children on board.

Once the Santa Special has arrived attention is drawn to the little train arriving from the other direction with a very special person onboard.

Photo: Karl Heath

Yes, you guessed it, Santa has commandeered *Dougal* for the festive season and the look on the children's faces as he left his train to join theirs, for the next part of the journey, warmed a very cold day.

*Opposite:* With Santa and his band of helpers on board distributing presents, *The Countess* prepares to depart on the final leg of the outward journey which on these weekends is to Castle Caereinion.

A Gala day departure, from 1999, and this vintage mixed train is going all the way to Welshpool.

Photo: Karl Heath

A mid–winter train weaves its way across the gently undulating landscape around Dolarddyn Crossing.

In September 2005 a plan to take a couple of shots of *Orion* passing over the crossing took an interesting twist.

Photo: Karl Heath

Just before the train was due by, this beautifully restored Stanley steam car arrived on the scene and turned to pull up alongside the crossing.

As the car passed by the driver asked me whether he would be in my picture if he drew up to the crossing.

To his surprise 'I certainly hope so' was my reply!

The train is photographed between the two crossings on the B4385 on a hazy winter's day. To the right the road heads for that at Dolarddyn and onwards to Llanfair. To the left it climbs to Castle Caereinion passing over the line at the station a quarter of a mile before reaching the village.

*The Earl* slows for a stop at Castle Caereinion having worked a goods train from Llanfair just like it would have done over a century ago.

With the exception of the two Santa weekends in December the railway is closed from the end of October until the beginning of April but there is no rest for the volunteers, especially those in the permanent way gangs.

They use this shutdown period to carry out repairs and maintenance of the track and here are re-ballasting the section at the Welshpool end of Castle Caereinion Station on a bitterly cold winter's morning.

The view from the station is spectacular taking in the Vale of Meifod, the Berwyns and on clear days I believe a distant view of Snowdon is possible.

Another couple of photographs taken on the evening of 31 August 2002 at Coppice Lane. Bathed in what appeared to be all that remained of that day's sunlight No.14 approaches the crossing summit.

The same train having crossed over the lane makes the sharp descent towards Sylfaen giving those passengers on the rear balcony a perfect view of the setting sun.

With Sylfaen in its sights *The Countess* coasts through the open countryside.

*Opposite:* Gala weekend trains run into the evening affording the opportunity for some twilight photography which can occasionally produce a very pleasing result.

Most of the railway's goods stock has been rebuilt in near original form and makes an impressive sight alongside the multi-national passenger coaches.

Gradient profiles made simple.

Photo: Karl Heath

In this distant view the 'uphill' section indicated can clearly be determined as *The Countess* takes a run at the final leg of the climb to the line's summit for Welshpool-bound trains.

Journeys end as the train arrives back at Raven Square on cool damp autumnal day…

...and here on a beautiful summer's day.

*Opposite:* Now it is time to unload those sacks from Llanfair.

At the end of the line is liquid refreshment for not only the engine but also the footplate crew. Having completed another photographic journey your photographer/author is also off for a brew and a slice of homemade cake at the superb station buffet at Llanfair Caereinion. I hope that this album will have encouraged you to join me and spend some time at this gem of a railway.